a lifetime of *Girlfriends*

moments of discovery

by Bonnie Jensen

BARBOUR
PUBLISHING

Bonnie would like to acknowledge the generous contribution of
Anita Wiegand to this little book of friendship.
She is not only a joy to work with, but a joy to befriend as well.

Scripture quotations marked TLB are taken from *The Living Bible* copyright © 1971. Used by permission of Tyndale House Publishers, Inc., Wheaton, Illinois 60189. All rights reserved.

Scripture quotations marked THE MESSAGE are taken from THE MESSAGE. Copyright © by Eugene H. Peterson 1993, 1994, 1995. Used by permission of NavPress Publishing Group.

Scripture quotations marked NIV are taken from the HOLY BIBLE, NEW INTERNATIONAL VERSION®. NIV®. Copyright © 1973, 1978, 1984 by International Bible Society. Used by permission of Zondervan Publishing House. All rights reserved.

Cover and interior images: Getty Images
Designed by Julie Doll.

Published by Barbour Publishing, Inc., P.O. Box 719, Uhrichsville, Ohio 44683,
www.barbourbooks.com

Our mission is to publish and distribute inspirational products offering exceptional value and biblical encouragement to the masses.

Member of the
Evangelical Christian
Publishers Association

Printed in China.
5 4 3 2

It is what we discover in each other on the journey of
friendship that opens our eyes of understanding.
By looking into the heart of a true friend, we see a reflection
of ourselves. . .and we learn things only they can teach us.

*A true friend
sticks by you.*

PROVERBS 18:24 THE MESSAGE

We had to be together every minute because we didn't want to miss the chance to make a memory.

On Friday afternoon there was only one question between friends: "Are you staying at my house, or am I staying at yours?"

sleepovers

Remember when
happiness consisted
of comfortable jeans,
a cute T-shirt, a
good friend, and a
cancelled gym class?

simplicity

good

Every day spent with a friend was a deposit into my "good memory" account.

perfect

Whatever is good and perfect comes to us from God.

JAMES 1:17 TLB

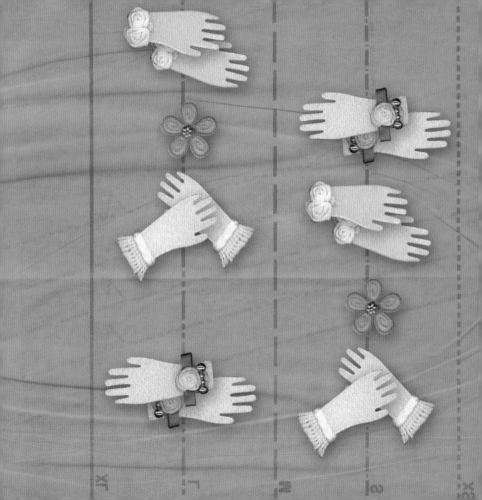

One of the most
beautiful qualities
of true friendship is
to understand and
be understood.
— *Seneca*

My friends have a
way of shining a whole
new light on things. . . .
I feel understood and
encouraged all at once.

For the perfect weekend,
all we needed was a good
friend, a good movie, and
all our favorite junk food.

A friend is a gift you give yourself.

–Robert Louis Stevenson

My friends were always honest with me. . . . I never had to finish out the school day not knowing there was broccoli from lunch stuck in my teeth.

Remember when we
were excited about
collecting key chains
even before we had any
keys to put on them?

Key chains

Were lockers really for books and supplies, or were they mini display cases for pictures of our best friends and favorite bands?

lockers

teens

Oh, the innocent girl
In her maiden teens
Knows perfectly well
What everything means.
—from "The Jeune Fille" by D. H. Lawrence

slumber parties

Slumber parties are the culmination of all things
girly—silliness, giggling, secrets, brushing hair,
painting fingernails, trying on clothes, calling boys
(only, of course, to scream and hang up as soon as
they answer)!

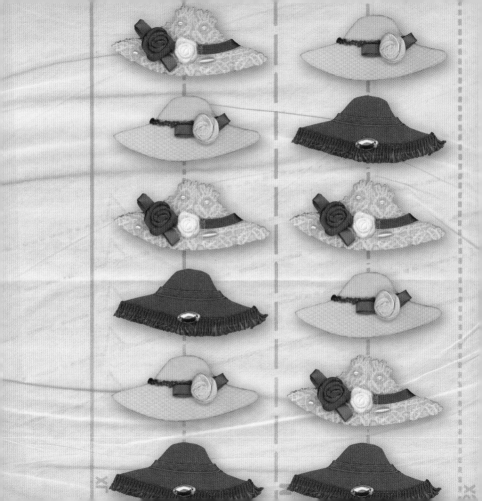

It's a girl thing:
Writing the name of the boy
who you dreamed of calling
your own over and over, as if
that somehow made your
secret crush more like reality.

Blemishes, braces,
bad hair, break-ups. . .
Wow! No wonder
friends were mandatory.

Remember when friends were
expected to know everything?...
"Does he like me?"
"What did he say?"
"Did he ask anyone to the dance?"

*Loyalty is what we seek
in friendship.*

—*Cicero*

Those were the days. . .
when a trip to the mall
could cure everything
from a bad test grade to
a broken heart.

Learning was the main
objective for going to
school, but seeing your
friends was really the
true and best reason.

love ya. . .

The greatest gift is a
portion of yourself.
—Ralph Waldo Emerson

like a sis

secrets

Keeping secrets will never go out of style.

compliments

A true friend will give you compliments freely
at the risk of feeling small.

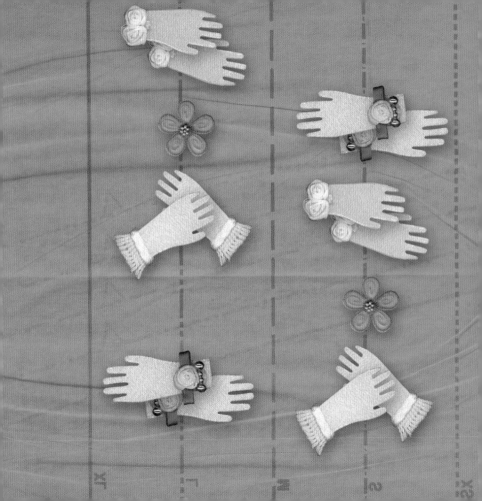

It occurred to me very early in life
that my friends were an invaluable
expression of God's love. They were
there for my first broken heart. . .
the loss of my favorite pet. . .
and the disappointment of having
no date for the prom.

I discovered how much I needed them—and I knew that the hugs, smiles, understanding, and support were all part of His care.

Even after seeing each other all day in school, I couldn't wait to get home to call my best friend.

Driving around in a car was the coolest thing ever.
It symbolized the first taste of freedom and made us feel
suddenly grown up. It felt, for an instant, as if we had wings.

Friendship is one of those true-blue
things in life—an accepting,
understanding, trusting, forgiving,
I'm-here-for-you kind of blessing.

It didn't matter where we were or what we were doing —being with friends made everything feel like it was the best place in the world.

Emotion-packed memories were part
of growing up—hellos and good-byes,
being hurt and making up,
disappointments and triumphs—it
was one of the most dramatic learning
curves in our lives. . .and that's one of
the greatest reasons why God made
friendship such an important part of
the process.

ups and downs

Don't let anyone think little of
you because you are young.
Be their ideal; let them follow
the way you teach and live; be
a pattern for them in your
love, your faith, and your
clean thoughts.

1 Timothy 4:12 TLB

ideals

believing

It's easier to believe in yourself when
you have a friend beside you saying,
"I believe in you, too."

future

Remember coordinating future goals with
your best friend so you didn't have to think
about being separated?

True friends understand
and overlook your
up-and-down moods.

What a great blessing is
a friend with a heart so
trusty you may safely
bury all your secrets in it.

—Seneca

*Friendship is a safety net
that seems to adjust in size,
according to your crisis!*

There is a small circle of people that we
surround ourselves with who become the safe
haven to which we run. . . . They're called friends.

Do I wear silver or gold, hat or no hat,
short sleeves or long sleeves, sneakers
or flip-flops. . .oh, the pressures!

Friends are
a reminder
that wishes
can come
true.

Five Things You Can Only Understand in Your Teenage Years:

. . .how critical it is to keep the phone line open (in case someone's trying to get through)

telephones

. . .how important it is to get a ride to
school with someone other than a parent
or a bus driver
. . .how much more productive it is to
study with friends as opposed to the quiet
confines of your own room
. . .how physically demanding it is to keep
your room clean
. . .how catastrophic a bad hair day truly is

bad hair days

passing notes

Remember writing notes that revealed your
most intimate thoughts and passing them to
your friend during class? (It was way more
fun than e-mail.)

malls

Our sense of direction was fairly developed in early
adulthood; we knew where every mall was within a
fifty-mile radius.

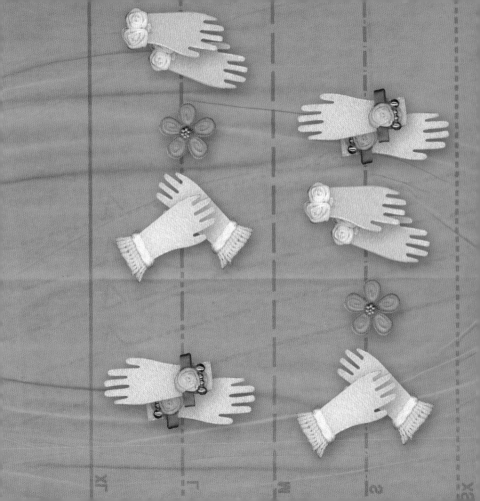

Remember when "who's who" represented a complete list of who's dating who, who's mad at who, and who broke up with who?

It's wonderful to be young!
Enjoy every minute of it!

ECCLESIASTES 11:9 TLB

We laughed (hysterically).
We giggled (for no reason).
We trusted (without reservation).
We accepted (without conditions).

Friends are life's little "pick-me-uppers."

Remember laughing until tears rolled down your face?
Going to the bathroom in groups of three?
Doing homework at the last minute?
Getting a haircut because it was "in"? . . .
Then wanting so badly to grow it "out"?

One cannot make the word "selfish" out of the word "friendship"— and that is just as it should be.

In the company of a
friend, anywhere feels
like home.

home

In my mind I've made a scrapbook. . .a collage of memories formed in the comfort of friendship.

memories

best friends

Two are better than one. . .if one falls down,
his friend can help him up.

ECCLESIASTES 4:9–10 NIV

forever

Hold tightly the memories made in the joy of
friendship.

We were so eager to do "grown-up" things...

shave our legs

wear makeup

drive a car

own a credit card

(Who knew some of these things
would prove to be dangerous?)

I remember my first love and, subsequently, my first heartbreak. It makes me smile to imagine my best friend scrambling to come up with a list of reasons why breaking up was a "good thing." I didn't feel like laughing. . .but she made me. (Now I know how important it was for me to oblige.)

Forever and for always
Runs to your rescue
Insists everything will be okay
Eases the "ouches" of life
No matter what (I'm here)
Delivers needed hugs
   (at just the right times)

Good friends make the best company.

A friend believes in your
dreams and cheers the loudest
when they come true.

When dreams come true at last, there is life and joy.

PROVERBS 13:12 TLB

Staying up all night went from
being hours of talking, laughing,
and doing each other's hair to hours
of reading, writing, and studying.
The common denominator: caffeine.
Lots of caffeine.

caffeine

I remember meeting a guy I
thought might be "the one."
It all depended, of course,
on whether or not my best
friend agreed.

guys

family

There was a time in high school when I wasn't sure if my house was home or if I had become an official member of my best friend's family—half of my personal belongings were at her house at any given time.

love

I have learned that to have a good friend is the purest of all God's gifts, for it is a love that has no exchange of payment.

—*Frances Farmer*

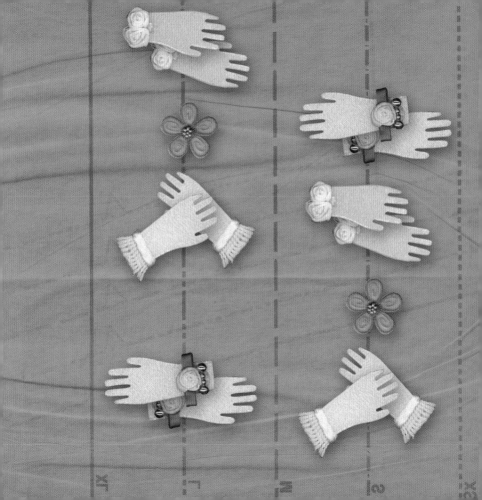

First-time experiences were less intimidating with a friend by your side.

It was unlikely that any of our "group" of girls would become makeup artists, but there were no limits to what we could do to each other in the realm of cosmetology.

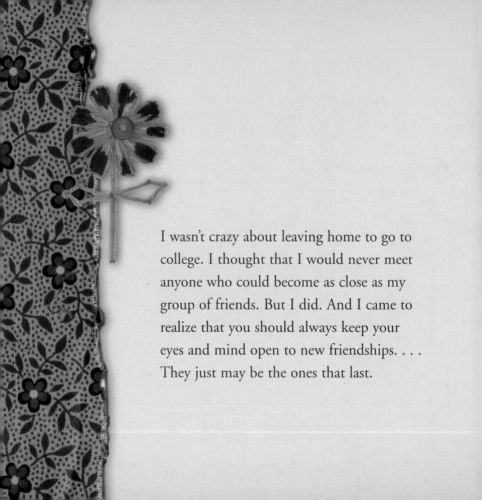

I wasn't crazy about leaving home to go to college. I thought that I would never meet anyone who could become as close as my group of friends. But I did. And I came to realize that you should always keep your eyes and mind open to new friendships. . . . They just may be the ones that last.

Let me tell thee, time is a very precious gift from God;
so precious that it's only given to us moment by moment.
—*Amelia Barr*

I was one who always strived so hard to be trendy in my hairstyle and the clothes that I bought. Can you remember the girls who had the courage to be different?

Remember the good old days when the most pressing issue you had to deal with for the day was a fashion emergency!

I joined the "drama" club. . . .
I thought the only prerequisite
was simply being female.

drama

Remember using the excuse that you had too much homework to avoid having to do chores, only to have a friend call ten minutes later and ask you to go to the mall? Drats!

priorities

boys, boys, boys

Didn't it seem like the boys you liked didn't like you and the boys you weren't interested in were interested in you? What was that all about? . . .

true friends

True friends are a sure refuge.

—*Aristotle*

I remember joining clubs and signing up for classes just to be with my friends. I never thought of it as peer pressure—it was more like a "de-stressor" because we got to spend more time together.

There are many things
that can be left unspoken
between friends, but two
words must never remain
silent—"I'm sorry."

One enemy is too many; a hundred friends too few.

—Anonymous

Silliness used to be mandatory when going out with your girlfriends. You had to be ready and willing to act goofy in public—goofier if there were cute boys around.

While growing up, there were a lot of things that seemed important, but having a best friend was priceless.

I never believed there was a difference between my dreams and what I could achieve. In my young mind, they were one and the same.

God can do anything, you
know—far more than you could
ever imagine or guess or request
in your wildest dreams!
EPHESIANS 3:20 THE MESSAGE

His guidance

A true friend is someone
you dare to dream out
loud with.

share your dreams

listen

Sometimes you just need a friend to listen without responding, to support you without judging.

be yourself

The rules of friendship are simple:
Be yourself.
Never put yourself first.

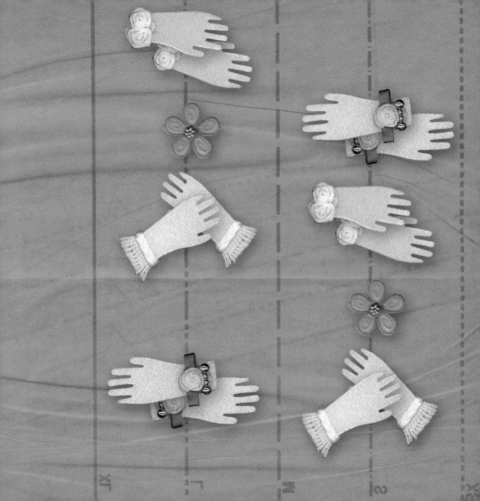

What was more exciting than prom? A trip to the salon for hair, nails, and makeup. . . and a dress that made you feel like a princess.

The memories I have of my friends are filed under "best times of my life," "most embarrassing moments," and "times I laughed the hardest."

From slumber
parties to proms. . .
from spelling bees to
final exams. . .
from bicycles to cars. . .
from innocent friendships
to lifelong friends.

The future belongs to
those who believe in the
beauty of their dreams.
—Eleanor Roosevelt